MANIFEST

[illegible]

in [illegible] Easy Steps

Linda West

First Edition

Dec 16, 2014

Contents

Prelude 1

CHAPTER 1: Decide What to Wish For 7

CHAPTER 2: The Triangle Process 11

CHAPTER 3: Getting into a High Frequency 15

CHAPTER 4: How to Make a Make-A-Wish Movie 21

CHAPTER 5: How to Keep That Loving Feeling 25

CHAPTER 6: Releasing to Receive 29

Final thoughts: 35

Prelude

Hi. I'm Linda West; nice to meet you!

Congratulations—you made it! If you are reading this, then you are in the master's class! You are ready to create your life instead of being pushed along with the daily current.

You are ready to be living your dreams! Sages have said throughout the years that when the student is ready, the teacher will appear...

So you must be ready for greatness, and that is something to be proud of. Good for you! You have earned the right to be told the inner secrets.

I'm going to tell you the formula my clients and I use to manifest our dreams and needs quickly.

What is manifestation? Simply stated…

Manifestation is channeling your wishes into reality.

After multitudes were made aware of the law of attraction by hits like *The Secret,* I noticed a demand for the how-to part that was never mentioned in the popular work.

People understood and believed in its message, but they didn't have any idea how to do it, which is similar to the idea that knowing the mechanics of riding a bike and actually *riding* a bike are two very different entities. That's why I wrote this book. I want to help you understand the true secrets that *The Secret* didn't tell you!

After you read this book, you will realize that you have been creating your whole life for the good or for the bad. You are in the driver's seat. So, where shall we go?

When I was five years old, I had a near-death experience. It gave me access to information that most people don't live to tell about. When I came back, I had a clear connection to the divine realm. I had a full understanding of the laws of frequencies at an intuitive level (we all do, but it gets slowly shut down as we grow into the matrix..

About fifteen years ago, I started dreaming about triangles and math and time. I started having visions of an angelic guide, White Eagle, who taught me nightly about the foundational sciences of the universe. I didn't understand the dreams nor did I have a passion for mathematics in anyway.

To be honest, I hated math and everything to do with the subject. I chose to major in English so I could stay *away* from math!

That said, when the dreams wouldn't go away, I decided I should start keeping track of them and write things down. It also seemed I was being called by a divine source to share something important.

In my effort to understand, I started reading books that I normally would never read or have any interest in. I read books on quantum physics, string theory, vibration and the Mayan Calendar. I ultimately began to formulate an understanding of the universal science of frequencies, which later would become my first book, *Ultimate Power: The Use of Frequency Attunement.*

I ended up winning a scholarship based on my work from famed cultural icon and scientist Terrence McKenna. I was asked to go into a rainforest with top scientists from around the world to do research on frequencies. It was a transformative experience that led to my understanding of the universal science of vibration, which was shown to me in the form of frequency attunement. After the book was published I went on to lecture every month on the new science of frequencies.

With the information I received through my dreams and the research I did in the rainforest, I was able to develop a way to actually show other people how to, step-by-step, create a wish that comes true.

In my effort to simplify this process, I developed my

5-Step Formula

for quick and easy manifestation.

When we are young, we tend to manifest things naturally because one of the most potent parts of the process is loving something and having passion for it. We have a lot of that as children and less of it as adults. So, cultivate those childlike moments—they bring you wonderful things and reduce your stress too.

One of the things I really wanted as a child was to own a restaurant. I was so consumed with it as a young girl that I decided to open one out of my basement in Buffalo when I was six. I made a sign and put it outside on the snow bank in front of our little house and called it "Blue Suede Shoes Cafe." I had daily customers despite the blizzard-like conditions.

I look back now and wonder about the kind of strange people who were coming to a six-year-old's basement restaurant. But that's another story. The important point is that I was building up to a greater future manifestation with this early childhood creation.

Unfortunately, I had reluctant landlords, i.e., my parents didn't like me running a restaurant out of our basement with my Barbie Burger Grill and Easy Bake Oven.

After one little fire, they shut down my business. Go figure.

Despite the fact that it was short-lived, I put that frequency out there and years later that frequency brought me the restaurant I have today.

After I channeled the book on frequencies and began to apply what I knew on how to manifest, I started manifesting things in my life. One of those things was the restaurant I bought and ran with two of my girlfriends for ten years. I manifested the restaurant that I had always wanted as a child and I did it using the same technique I'm going to teach you now.

I didn't put any of my own money down. Heck, I was a single mom at that time and barely had money for the electric bill let alone to go investing in a restaurant.

Remember, if I can do it, you can do it.

I didn't know how my dream was going to come about for me and you won't know how it's going to come about for you either, but` it will come in a beautiful, amazing way, and of that I can assure you!

After reading these steps, if you would like a more in-depth understanding of all these tips, they are available in my extended version of this book,

"Secrets The Secret Never Told You"

I also offer many client stories of manifestation for you to learn from.

CHAPTER 1

Decide What to Wish For

Your first step toward manifesting your dream is deciphering what really gets you excited and passionate enough to manifest it! Sounds fun, right?!

In fact, figuring out what really makes you happy and what you really want in your heart and spirit might be the hardest part of the entire process of manifestation.

So now I'm going to get your gears going with this question: *What is it that you could bring into your life right now that would truly make your spirit and your heart happy?*

I urge you to go after your dreams—little dreams, big dreams, passions and love. These are the things that will bring you joy and a life of purpose and happiness. Keep dreaming!

Because it is very common for people to have resistance to even searching for what they really love and what would make them happy, I developed this simple exercise to help you.

Please take a moment to try this now, and then write down afterwards everything that comes to your mind.

Step 1, Exercise 1: Figuring Out What You Want

1. Sit down in a quiet place and take three deep breaths—one for mind, one for body, one for spirit.
2. 2) When you are comfortable and relaxed, I want you to imagine:

Imagine...

Manifest

You were just given $300 million dollars as a

gift. Now check in with your triangle.

Ask your mind what it wants to do with $300 million dollars.

Ask your body what it wants to do with $300 million dollars.

Now ask your spirit what dream it wants to follow with the
freedom allowed by that $300 million dollars.

Now that you have all the money in the world,

what do you want?

CHAPTER 2

The Triangle Process

Now that you have figured out what you love and want to manifest, we have to go see the judges.

You have to be clear about what you want.

The reason you have to be clear is because you will not manifest what you want unless *all three parts of you* wants it.

Sometimes we shut out voices we don't want to hear but they are trying to communicate with us.

In the *West,* we tend to listen primarily to our mind and not as much to the voices of our bodies or spirit hearts. However, we are working with the third dimension, and thus the triangle. Therefore, what we manifest always depends on an agreement between the three parts of ourselves that make up our complete self.

Very often you will find that some part of your triangle has resistance. This means a part of you is unsure. Don't fight that.

That voice is protecting you and looking out for an integral part of your happiness.

As much as you may want to leap straight into your dream, sometimes taking single steps toward it is better. I know you've heard that life is about enjoying the journey and that is very true. Each step is to be savored just like a bite from a succulent meal. After all, life is made up of beautiful steps and moves. Don't hurry up the game, friends—revel in the joy of playing!

Sometimes a dream takes steps. This is not because you can't manifest large things. The simple fact is that change is scary to most humans.

Big leaps mean big changes. Your life changes when things change. Things change when you change; sometimes jobs, sometimes friends, sometimes marriages....

Even when those things that change are for the better, it can still be scary.

When you go to manifest something, you need to realize that you are working with three parts of yourself. Those three parts will each be affected differently by the changes that come into your life.

These are like three little judges. We have our own little congressional system and balancing act going on, except in our case, it's the mind, the body, and the spirit.

Whether you like it or not, you must pay attention to what each one of them is saying.

You won't manifest anything or pull it into the third dimension without all three parts of yourself agreeing on it. Things manifest from the frequency realm via the sacred triangle in the third dimension.

Ultimately you are using six-dimensional geometry to do this so that it can manifest.

In my practice, very often my clients get in their own way because they don't really want what they're trying to manifest. Or more precisely, a part of them doesn't want what the other two parts want...

That's when you realize you better listen to all three parts of you! It only takes one dissenter to stop something from manifesting!

All three parts of you have a voice and a choice in what you create. You can't ignore any part of you. However, you can often talk a reluctant side of yourself into something by scaling it down to a smaller step toward your goal.

If you find yourself blocked and not moving toward your dream, see if you can pull back and take a smaller step.

For example, I want to write a book but I'm feeling blocked. This is a huge ordeal. How do I unblock this feeling?

I'll think of a smaller step to take. What if I begin with ten minutes a day of writing? I do a quick Triangle Check and bingo, no resistance to ten minutes.

Thus I've found my starting step. I will begin writing ten minutes a day and someday I will have a finished book! (This is in fact how I was able to write my first book when my son was a baby and I had so little time to myself.)

Exercise 2: The Triangle Check

As I have mentioned, in my private practice, I have noticed the biggest problem people face in manifesting is wishing too big.

In this process, you take what you think you want and run it by the three judges: mind, body and spirit. We ask each of them for input on this dream.

Take a moment now to quiet yourself and to check in with your triangle about the goal you identified in the first exercise. Ask each part of you how it feels. How does your body feel about it, how does your head think about it and how does your spirit react about it coming true?

Is there any resistance?

Are all three parts of you ready for this now?

Ask yourself some questions and try to pinpoint the truth for yourself.

Can you scale it down in any way where you feel more comfortable?

CHAPTER 3

Getting into a High Frequency

So how are YOU feeling?

Are you ready to move ahead with your wish?

Are you so ready that if it came to you tomorrow, you'd be totally happy about it?

If you can truthfully answer *yes,* then you're ready.

Good, because we are going to go manifest it, and sometimes it happens right away. I very often have seen things manifest within 24 hours.

Conversely, at other times, it takes a little longer than you would imagine to manifest because the pieces have to be put into place. However, signs should appear quickly to show you that the message has been received. Look for synchronicities, co-incidences and symbols.

In Step 1, you identified what you want and made sure that all three parts of you are in agreement.

We are ready to move on to Step 2 in the process of creation.

Step 2: Get yourself into the highest frequency possible because like attracts like.

Good things come on good vibrations.

To manifest quickly, stay in the highest frequency possible all the time. This is a discipline that will serve you the greatest of any other secrets I give you. Stay high frequency and all good things naturally flow to you.

Do you know what a high frequency is? Some examples of a high frequency is anytime you're feeling good, like when you hear birds singing or little kids laughing. High frequencies live wherever love is emanating from you or when you're bouncing off the walls with joy!

Simply put, the higher the frequency, the more divine, happy and good it feels.

The science of frequencies can get kind of complicated, but to simplify things, just remember high frequencies make you feel good, so you should always move toward them.

Conversely, low frequencies make you feel bad, i.e., when you get sick, gain weight, lose your job, interact with mean people. Whenever you identify a low-frequency, you should move away from it.

The way you move away from a low frequency can be as simple as walking out the door (such is the case when the low frequency is your mother-in-law!).

Seriously, though, when you can't just walk away from a low vibe situation, you need to do it *energetically*.

Vibrationally, you do this by raising your frequency above it, by going to the next highest frequency you can get to.

If the foundational science of frequencies interests you, then you should check out my first book where I go into the complete understanding of the science of frequencies and the law of attunement, *Ultimate Power*. Or you can check out any of my free videos on this at MorningMayan on YouTube.

I'm planning the release of my complete book On frequencies in early 2015.

The next simple part of frequencies you will have to understand is how frequencies interact with each other.

Similar frequencies are drawn to other frequencies like themselves. Like attracts like. Like frequencies attract like frequencies by the law of attraction.

To sum it up, everything has a frequency, but what we are looking for is the high frequencies, which make you feel good.

It's very important to launch a high frequency wish or goal off of another high frequency vibration.

Don't go practicing this technique when you're in fear, doubt, sadness or illness. You have to wait until you get into an authentically happy place or you somehow boost yourself into

a fake happy place, which also counts as a high frequency. What you're feeling is what you're feeling—it doesn't matter how you got there.
After you get into a high frequency, we do the exercise on manifesting.

Because of the law of affinity, remember to make a wish when you're in a high frequency!

A few years ago, I was in Big Sur. I was on a big tree swing in front of my friend's cottage. The swing was one of the coolest things I'd ever been on because it swung out over the highway and valley that also overlooked the Pacific Ocean.

Every time I would swing out over the roadway, people driving by would look up and be totally surprised to see me and wave up to me because it looked like I had fallen out of the sky!

This for some reason made me ecstatically happy and joyful! The child-like experience of hiding and then popping through the clouds and surprising people driving on the road was exhilarating!

I know what makes me happy might not make you happy, but I realized at that moment of silly joy, that it was a make-a-wish moment. I was so ecstatically happy I was hitting a very high frequency!

When you are in a high frequency, it is time to send out your wishes. A high frequency means it's make-a-wish time!

Once my make-a-wish time was identified, I followed up with the next step.

If you remember nothing else from this book, let it be that every time you get in a super happy place, remember it's wish time, so send out those wishes, baby!

As you'll see, like attracts like by the law of affinity, but it's what we *FEEL* that creates the vibrations that set up the pattern for the matching light vibrations to integrate with.

We FEEL things into existence in the third dimension.

We build a foundational house for the dream to manifest by loving it to ourselves with a high frequency.

Ultimately, we're talking about source key energy that you want to match up with or emulate. I found that one of the easiest, sure-fire ways of getting into a high frequency is to read comedy and watch comedy, and when you're laughing, you're officially in a high frequency. Then while you're laughing... manifest!

I also walk in nature or do something artistic to get myself into a high frequency. If I'm not feeling up, a sure-fire way to raise my frequency is a hot yoga class. I know what works for me, but you need to discover your passions yourself! People with passions are happy people. People without passions are sad.

Look around and see the truth of that for yourself. The one common trait all addicts in rehab have is a lack of passion. It's what we lose that makes us grow up and be old. Cultivate your passions.

Savor your dreams and dare to have a life worth living by

going after them one by one! Don't be bored to death and drink yourself to an early grave. Please, the world needs you.

Begin to look around in your life and search avidly for things that bring you joy, and become aware when you enter those special high-frequency moments.

When you have identified without a doubt that you're in a high frequency and it's make-a-wish time, then it's time to move on to Step 3 and make that wish to the universe in the form of a movie.

CHAPTER 4

How to Make a Make-A-Wish Movie

Now that you've done Step One and you are able to identify what exactly it is that you want, and you've done Step 2 and have yourself in a make-a-wish high frequency, NOW is the time to use this technique.

Wherever you are, excuse yourself for a moment, or if you're by yourself in a high frequency already, then you are ready to go.

This step involves making up a movie in your head with real players, imagining what everybody would say, what you would be hearing, and more importantly, what you would be feeling.

Some of the things you should be feeling if you're creating the movie realistically are joy, *hooray*, and *oh my gosh, my wish is coming true right now.*

Your goal is to create such a believable movie inside your head by using as many senses and as much creativity as possible that you actually start to get excited about it *as if* it were real.

You actually attempt to fake yourself out.

You fake yourself into a feeling by creating a movie exactly as you'd like to see it playing out in your life, to the point that you get excited about the possibility of it, and the truth of it. When you actually feel excited or happy, your movie has been successful!

Now that you are feeling the realness of it, try to hold onto that feeling for as long as possible.

Attempt to hold the feeling as if it were actually occurring.

The science on this says that you need exactly sixteen seconds to send out a frequency wave. Your goal is to feel that fake feeling of accomplishment and getting what you want for sixteen seconds or more...

As you're creating this movie inside you, what you're actually doing is creating a vibrational pattern to send out to the universe that you want *MATCHED,* (i.e., the law of attraction, law of affinity, like attracts like) so in this movie, you need to use all parts of yourself. It's vital that you use all five senses to play out this movie in your mind.

Imagine it in the *PRESENT* tense—what exactly do you want to happen? Imagine what it would look like if this little miracle, this wish, was coming true and it was taking place in your life right now?

Most likely, the scenario you're creating is going to have other players, and it will probably involve people saying things to you, such as, “Congratulations, you finally got the promotion!” or “That girl you like is on the phone for you!” Perhaps even, “There’s somebody at the door who wants to talk to you about giving you that school grant.”

It’s going to be a fake movie you make up, but it is still the movie you want to see take place in your life in the *PRESENT.*

I like to get in a private place and close my eyes, imagining it just like a Hollywood blockbuster.

The most important part of the whole movie is the feeling that it creates in you. The feeling in your gut is the frequency-maker, which drives your manifestation and pulls in your wish.

Feeling joy for something is the *most important* part—it’s how we create things.

In this case, you are creating a fake feeling that will send out vibrations to pull in the real thing.

It is the art of believing as if it already happened.

Some people will call this faith.

Once you are getting to the feeling place, and feeling good and excited, you will start to feel it slowly dissipate.

The fakeness will begin to show its ugly head. That’s perfectly okay. That’s normal.

Since we know that one of the keys to manifesting is how much energy, or feeling, that we put into feeling *as if*, we can conclude logically that the longer we can keep the feelings going, the more likely it appears.

Sixteen seconds is good, but more is better!

And that leads us directly to Step 4.

CHAPTER 5

How to Keep That Loving Feeling

We have already identified the fact that the longer you keep a feeling going, the more power you put behind it. Those frequencies being sent out are going to find the matching frequencies, and the stronger the frequency output, the stronger the attraction quality.

The next step involves keeping the feeling going so you can maximize your attraction pull power.

We need to keep the feelings from the movie that you made up in your head, albeit the fake movie, revved up and powerful. As I mentioned, it takes at least 16 seconds to form a vibrational wave pattern. The longer we can keep that pattern generating, the quicker it will manifest in your life.

To keep these fake feelings motoring up, we're going to use a little trick I came up with to extend the feeling so you have a stronger vibrational push.

This trick involves imagining bringing in people that you love that will be happy for you if your wish comes true.

Jesus mentions when two or more pray together that miracles happen because the divine force joins them. I guess it's the Holy Trinity coming true, so once again we are dealing with the triangle.

Consequently, if you imagine that you're telling somebody who really loves you that your wish just came true, they actually vibrationally join into the creation of that wish with you. Now with the two of you wishing together for this wonderful creation, the divine force of the Holy Trinity is enacted and it joins into creating your wish too!

Now you have the triangle working for you!

The way you're going to use this is right after you accomplish Step 3 and create the movie in your head. The movie gets you into the feeling of, "Wow, this is awesome; this is what it would be like if it were truly taking place."

As I mentioned,

Your goal is to hold that fake feeling for as long as possible and at least for sixteen seconds.

As we know, this feeling will begin to dissipate, and when it does fade, this is when you *imagine* telling the story to somebody that you care about who would be happy for you.

Retell the story, and, more importantly, relive the happy feelings and *feel* them.

You make the sensations real again for you (remember, fake it before you make it!). Like attracts like with the law of affinity.

For example, you might imagine telling your mother some great news. You got the promotion you were hoping for, you got the grant you were applying for, you got the date that you'd been dreaming of...imagine telling your mother or your close friend and envision how happy they will be for you.

While you are conjuring this, the feelings of their joy will combine with the feelings of *your* joy and rev up those feelings again, which will create more happy high frequencies. Whoopee! Try and keep it going for sixteen seconds.

At this point, throw in another good friend. Tell it to them, too!

Tell it to Grandma. Tell it to everyone. They will say, "I am so proud of you! I am so happy for you!"

And you? You will answer, "I am so happy, too! I can't believe how lucky I am. This is the greatest day of my life!"

Bingo.

You are now smack in the middle of creating those feeling frequencies that are flowing out into the universe to get you those feelings for real. To get you what you want for real. To get you all that joy and success for real and to get you the ability to tell that story for real, to the same real people someday.

This is what creating your life is all about.

Do not just walk into each day like somebody on autopilot.

Create your life, make it happen the way you want it to happen. I know you can do it.

CHAPTER 6

Releasing to Receive

Okay, we are rounding the bend to the last step, and this truly is going to be the easiest.

To recap:

Step 1: We figured out what we really want.

Step 2: We've gotten ourselves into a high frequency.

Step 3: We have imagined a movie in our head and made it feel real.

Step 4: We extended those fake feelings by pretending to tell somebody, who loves us and will share in our happiness, that our dream came true.

We've reached the final step.

Step 5: Letting go with gratitude.

So here we are, at the end, and you're about to manifest

what you want. The last step involves letting go and being grateful.

It's very important to realize that things come in on frequency levels, so your only job from here on out is to stay away from any thoughts of worry that your manifestation might not come true.

This is where it gets a bit tricky and you're going to have to really go with your gut on the truth of this. If you're really just in love, jazzed and passionate about something but not *worried*, then that's the best place to be.

If you feel really good about your dream manifesting, but just haven't seen anything show up yet, it is okay to redo the 5 steps when you find yourself in an extra high frequency.

If you're freaking out and afraid and think it's not working, then it's not working.

Worry is a low-frequency. You need to let go. Be cool.

Flow with a divine nonchalance and have faith that what you want is arriving in just the perfect time. Stay in a grateful place *as if* it's already arrived.

Stay in a high frequency.

Your only job now is to get out of any low frequency thoughts or feelings of fear and find a way back up into the high frequency of faith.

This comes down to letting it go, and letting it come in, and being thankful for it *as if* it had already happened.

Often when people really want something, they can't help but be concerned that it might not come in. Yet this is the leap you have to take. It's called a leap of faith. You have to let it go.

I think one of the most important parts of this step is being grateful and thankful.

I often thank God for things that I haven't seen show up in my life yet, as well as for the things that have shown up in my life.

In this way, I keep saying to the divine universe that I have faith—the universe is already aware of my dreams and bringing them in. I'm already grateful.

Appreciation. It's a good thing. It helps being grateful.

Not to mention, being grateful is a very high frequency!

Okay, so you said thank you to the universe for sending it to you and released it into the hands of the divine.

You've done everything you could do, including remembering to maintain a high frequency.

Some ways to accomplish raising your frequency are to go out in nature, dance, play with pets and continue to do things that make you happy and bring you up to a good high frequency feeling place. The high frequencies always magnetize things to you quicker.

A common question I get in my lectures is, "How long do I have to wait before my wish shows up?"

As I said before, when you get very clear and you really love something and you don't have fear around it and you are enthusiastic about it, then it can show up immediately. I've seen things show up within 24 hours—sometimes sooner.

Conversely, sometimes you have to wait for the divine order of things to fall into place.

Sometimes certain things in the universe, or people, have to be moved around and put into position for your wish to manifest, and that can take time. Especially if it involves other people, then you also have to deal with their timing.

If what you want isn't manifesting right away, it just may be that the timing is not right. I know it sounds cliché but the universe works that way, too.

I would suggest as a hint, if you're not seeing your manifestation come through right away, to retry the whole five steps when you are in a high frequency. Run through the process again and send it out again—not in a stressful, fearful way, but just when you identify a high frequency moment. Send out another mini version of the wish.

The other thing I would do is go back and recheck and make sure that you're not wishing for something that's too big a step *for you* (according to your own triangle).

Re-examine and see if there is any part of the wish that you are having a bit of resistance to. If yes, perhaps you can start with trying to manifest a slightly smaller step.

I know you can do it!

I hope that this book helped you understand your amazing ability to use frequencies and your power to create.

I believe in you!

Go forth and manifest all that you

love, my friends!

Final thoughts:

When you turn the page, Amazon will give you the opportunity to rate this book and share your thoughts through an automatic feed to your Facebook and Twitter accounts. If you believe your friends would get something valuable out of this book, I would be honored if you tell them your thoughts.

If you feel particularly strong about the contributions this book made to your manifesting success, I'd be eternally grateful if you would post a review on Amazon. Just click here and it will take you directly to the page. I thank you.

Please visit me at my website MorningMayan.com

where I have the rest of my books and other tools that can help you manifest, including, for a limited time only, the availability to work with me as a coach.

Contact me directly at MorningMayan.com for info on upcoming events, new books or coaching.

If you would like to learn more about the basic science of frequencies, please get my book on Amazon -

Ultimate Power: The Universal Power of Love

And if you're really a frequency fan, look for my new complete book on frequencies due out in 2015.

If you're interested in manifesting your perfect divine body and shape, please check out my diet book that released me from weight issues.

The California Diet

Please also follow me on YouTube as: MorningMayan where I have lots of free videos on how to manifest and understand frequencies.

For complete info, go to MorningMayan.com

Please come over and join me socially on Facebook and Twitter as *MorningMayan.*

Linda West's newest release is available soon in paperback and e-book. *The Secrets the Secret Never Told You* is an extended version of *Manifest in 5 Easy Steps,* including real client stories to learn from.